When Mother Lets Us Cook

A Book of Simple Receipts for Little Folks

by

Mrs. Constance Fuller (Wheeler) Johnson

APPLEWOOD BOOKS
Bedford, Massachusetts

When Mother Lets Us Cook

was originally published in

1908

9781429014427

Thank you for purchasing an Applewood book.
Applewood reprints America's lively classics—
books from the past that are still of interest
to the modern reader.
For a free copy of
a catalog of our
bestselling
books,
write
to us at:
Applewood Books
Box 365
Bedford, MA 01730
or visit us on the web at:
For cookbooks: foodsville.com
For our complete catalog: awb.com

Prepared for publishing by HP

WHEN MOTHER LETS US COOK

When you bake a small thing, have the oven hot,
But for baking big things cool it off a lot.

WHEN MOTHER LETS US COOK

BOOK OF SIMPLE RECEIPTS FOR LITTLE FOLK WITH
IMPORTANT COOKING RULES IN RHYME TOGETHER
WITH HANDY LISTS OF THE MATERIALS AND
UTENSILS NEEDED FOR THE PREP-
ARATION OF EACH DISH

By CONSTANCE JOHNSON

ILLUSTRATED

NEW YORK
MOFFAT, YARD & COMPANY
1919

Copyright, 1908, by
MOFFAT, YARD & COMPANY
NEW YORK

All rights reserved

Published, September, 1908
Reprinted, May, 1909
Reprinted, December, 1909
Fourth Printing, November, 1910
Ninth Printing, March, 1915
Tenth Printing, February, 1916
Eleventh Printing, May, 1917
Twelfth Printing, June, 1919

TO MARY ABIGAIL'S FATHER,
WHO WILL DOUBTLESS HAVE TO PROVE
MANY A PUDDING.

TABLE OF CONTENTS

RECEIPTS

(For chafing-dish or saucepan)

	PAGE
BOILED EGGS	3
BOILED RICE	4
JELLY WARM-OVER	5
CREAM SAUCE	7
SCRAMBLED EGGS	8
APPLE SAUCE	9
STEWED FRUITS	11–14
SWEET SAUCES	15–17
CURLYLOCKS PUDDING	18
SWEET OMELET	21
CEREAL CAKES	23
PAN CAKES	24
BAKED STEWED PEARS	27

BAKING RECEIPTS

BAKED POTATOES	28
BAKED APPLES	29
NEST EGGS	30
TAPIOCA PUDDING	31
SCALLOPED FISH	33
RICE PUDDING	35
CUP CUSTARD	37
CHICKEN CUSTARD	39
BROWN BETTY	41

TABLE OF CONTENTS

	PAGE
Meat Loaf	43
Birthday Cake	45
Hilda's Johnny Cake	49
Blueberry Muffins	51
Katy's Gingerbread	53
Gingerbread Pudding	55
Tea-Party Biscuit	57
Saturday Cookies	59

USEFUL ODDS AND ENDS

Junket	61
School Sandwiches	63
Fairy Salad	64
Lemonade	65
Cottage Cheese	67
Clam Broth	69
Beef Tea	71
Milk Toast	72
Blackberry Bread	75
Angel Hash	76
Jelly Whip	77
Mock Wine Jelly	78
Tea	81
Cocoa	83
Popcorn Balls	86
Popcorn Patties	87
Candied Orange-Peel	88
Rainy-Day Fudge	90
Molasses Candy	92
Peppermints	94

TABLE OF CONTENTS

RULES

	PAGE
THINGS TO HAVE	1
WITCH'S TEST	2
MILK RULE	6
READY RULE	10
THINGS TO REMEMBER	14
WAITING RULE	20
BAKING RULE	26
SPOONFULS AND CUPFULS	32
STRAW TEST	36
WETS AND DRYS	42
OVEN DOORS	48
SIFTING AND STIRRING	56
BREAD AND BUTTER RULE	62
PS AND QS	66
SIMMERING RULE	70
RULE FOR SERVING COLD	74
BOILING RULE	80
CANDY RULE	84

PREFACE

To make something that we can eat! Surely it is always delightful to do this, and never quite so nice as when it is a stormy day, and one is—well—ten or twelve years old. My aim has been to give in this little book a few simple rules and receipts, which may serve as a beginning, and help small folks to have their fun without troubling mother and the cook too much; yet I trust that these directions may prove useful to them even when they are grown-up housekeepers.

The selection is made with a view to economy and a child's diet.

THINGS TO HAVE

Tablespoons, teaspoons, measuring cup,
Bowls, plates, knives, all polished up.
Egg-beater, lifting knife, baking tin,
Sauce-pans, bread-board, rolling-pin;
A double-boiler, a chafing-dish,
A wooden spoon I know you'll wish.
A flour sifter, a cutter, too;
A clock to show when the cooking 's through.
An apron to do the cooking in,
And hands scrubbed clean before you begin!

THE WITCH'S TEST

Put eggs in cold water to test them for food.
If they float they are bad, if they sink they are
   good.
And some people say that an egg is all right
If you hold it up close to a flame that is bright
And look through it endwise and still see a light.

BOILED EGGS

Fresh eggs   Saucepan
Boiling water

Never boil eggs that are not perfectly fresh; cook them some other way.

Put your fresh eggs, with their shells on, into a deep saucepan.

Fill the saucepan with water that is actually boiling, and see that the eggs are covered.

Take the pan from the stove and cover it. It may be brought to the dining room table, and the eggs will cook until you are ready to eat them.

Boiled eggs are better cooked in water that does not continue to boil;—but be sure that the water is boiling hard, when first poured over the eggs.

Three minutes will be enough for soft boiled eggs, fifteen for hard.

Serve at once in a covered dish, or wrapped in a clean table napkin.

BOILED RICE

1 cup rice	Measuring cup
3 quarts boiling water	Sieve
	Teaspoon
1 teaspoonful salt	Deep saucepan
	Fork

Measure 1 cupful of rice. Pick it over carefully so that there will be no yellow grains or specks of dirt left in it.

Then put the rice into a sieve or strainer and wash it. You can do this under the kitchen faucet or by pouring a pitcherful of cold water over the rice.

Put 3 quarts of hot water into a deep saucepan on the stove (the pan should have a cover) and when the water boils pour in the rice very slowly, and add 1 teaspoonful of salt.

Stir it a few times with a fork and then put the cover on the pan, and let the rice boil hard for about twenty minutes, or until it is soft.

Try a little with a fork when you think it is done.

Drain the water off by pouring rice and all into your sieve.

This is the best way to cook rice.

JELLY WARM-OVER

3 tablespoonfuls currant jelly
Cold beef or mutton
Pepper and salt
French mustard

Saucepan or chafing-dish
Spoons

If you have any cold beef or mutton left over from yesterday, cut it into rather thick slices.

Take your saucepan and put it on a hot part of the stove.

Put in your saucepan 1 heaping tablespoonful of butter, and as soon as it is melted add ½ teaspoonful of salt and a pinch of red pepper, mixing it well with a spoon. If you like, add 1 teaspoonful of French mustard.

Stir into this 3 generous tablespoonfuls of currant jelly.

When it is all smoking hot and well mixed, add your slices of meat.

Cook for a few more minutes until the meat is heated through and has absorbed some of the sauce.

Serve in a hot dish at once. Be sure to pour all the jelly sauce over the meat.

MILK RULE

For cooking milk two rules I tell,—
Milk quickly burns, so stir it well;

Or cook it in a double pot,—
It curdles where the stove's too hot.

CREAM SAUCE FOR ALL SORTS OF THINGS

1 tablespoonful flour	Saucepan or chafing-dish
1 tablespoonful butter	Spoon
1 cupful milk	Measuring cup
1 teaspoonful salt	
¼ teaspoonful pepper	

Put 1 tablespoonful of butter into a saucepan, and put the saucepan on the stove.

When the butter is melted add 1 tablespoonful of flour.

Stir every minute, for it burns easily.

When the butter and flour are frothy and well mixed, pour in 1 cup of milk or cream, drop by drop, stirring with the other hand.

Do this quickly, but be very careful not to let any lumps form; the stirring is to prevent this, and also to keep the sauce from burning.

Cook it till it boils up, and then stir in 1 teaspoonful of salt and ¼ teaspoonful of pepper.

The sauce is now ready for use.

This is enough for a dish for three people. It can be used with warmed-over meats, fish, toast, or sliced hard-boiled eggs.

SCRAMBLED EGGS FOR THREE

5 eggs	Egg beater
1 cup milk	Saucepan or chafing-dish
1 tablespoonful butter	Teaspoon
1 teaspoonful salt	Tablespoons
½ teaspoonful pepper	

Break 5 eggs into a bowl, being careful not to drop in any shells.

Add 1 teaspoonful of salt and ½ of pepper.

Beat for a minute with an egg-beater.

Add 1 cup of milk and beat a little longer.

Have a saucepan (you can also use a chafing-dish) on a hot part of the stove; put into it 1 tablespoonful of butter and let it melt.

Pour in the mixture and stir slowly.

Pretty soon the egg will begin to stick to the bottom of the pan; keep scraping it off as you stir.

When most of the mixture is thick and lumpy, the scramble is done.

Do not let it get hard.

Serve right away on hot plates; it is very nice to have some hot slices of toast ready and pour the mixture over them.

APPLE SAUCE

Apples	Saucepan
Sugar	Sharp knife
Butter	Apple-corer
Spices	Strainer or sieve
	Bowl

Choose some nice hard cooking apples, core them, and peel them with a sharp knife.

Cut them in quarters and lay these in a deep saucepan.

Sprinkle the apples with granulated sugar, allowing 1 cup for 6 good-sized apples, and add to this 2 tablespoonfuls of mixed spices, cloves, cinnamon, ginger, and so forth. If you do not like spices you need not put this in.

Pour into the saucepan 1 cup of cold water, and set the pan on a warm part of the stove.

The apples should cook for about fifteen minutes, until they are quite soft and the water is partly boiled away, leaving a syrup.

Take a coarse sieve or strainer, put 1 tablespoonful of butter in the bottom of it, and strain the applesauce into a bowl.

Push it through the strainer with a spoon if necessary.

Set the bowl in a cool place, and serve the apple sauce cold with milk or cream.

READY RULE

This rule above all others heed:—
Have ready everything you need.

Before you start be sure to read
The whole receipt, then work with speed.

STEWED FRUITS

When stewing fruits, do not let them boil hard. They should only simmer.

Cover the fruit with cold water and add sugar if the fruit is sour.

The saucepan should be put at the back of the stove and the fruit cooked until tender. This often takes from 2 to 3 hours.

Never use tin pans to cook fruit.

STEWED PRUNES

1 pound prunes   Saucepan

Put your prunes into an agate saucepan, and cover them with cold water, allowing 1 quart of water to each pound of prunes.

Put the pan at the back of the stove.

Cook until the prunes are tender, which will take about 2½ hours.

Try them with a fork to see if they are soft, and when done turn into a bowl to cool.

This is enough for 6 people.

They are good served with a little cream.

Dried fruits are cooked like prunes. A little sugar may be added to the water if you like it better.

STEWED RHUBARB

Rhubarb	Measuring cup
1 cup sugar	Saucepan
	Knife

Select tender stalks of rhubarb.

Cut off the green tops with a sharp knife and throw them away.

Cut the stalks into pieces about 1 inch long.

When you have cut enough to fill a quart measure put the pieces in a double boiler and barely cover them with cold water.

Set the pot at the back of the stove to simmer for several hours.

When you think the rhubarb is tender, try it with a fork.

Add 1 cup of granulated sugar to each quart of rhubarb.

Put the pot on a hot part of the stove and let the mixture boil hard for two minutes.

Pour into a dish to cool.

This is enough for 6 people.

Peaches, apricots, oranges, pears, apples, berries, and so forth can all be stewed in the same way. Berries will not take so long to cook. Large fruits should be peeled.

THINGS TO REMEMBER

16 tablespoons make one cup
If milk or water fill it up;
It takes but 8, heaped full and high,
If what you measure 's fine and dry.

SWEET SAUCES

RASPBERRY SAUCE

¼ cup sugar	Vegetable masher
1 cup raspberries	2 bowls
⅓ cup cream	Cheese cloth
	Measuring cup
	Fork
	Egg beater

Measure one cupful of ripe raspberries, pick them over carefully, and wash them if necessary.

Put the raspberries in a bowl with ¼ of a cupful of granulated sugar.

Stand them for ¾ of an hour in a warm room.

Spread a piece of cheesecloth over a bowl and pour the raspberries and sugar and all the raspberry juice into the cheesecloth.

Fold the cheesecloth over, so that the berries will be in a sort of bag, and mash them with a wooden masher until all the juice and fine pulp have gone through the cheesecloth into the bowl.

Put ⅓ of a cup of cream into another bowl and whip it with an egg-beater until very thick.

Pour the raspberry juice over it and mix carefully with a fork.

This can be served with ice cream, plain cake, cold rice, hominy, farina, custards, etc.

HOT CHOCOLATE SAUCE

2 cups sugar
1 cupful hot water
2 tablespoonfuls cocoa
Boiling water
1 teaspoonful vanilla

Sauce pan
Measuring cup
Tablespoon
Teaspoon

Measure 2 tablespoonfuls of cocoa and put them in a cup with 3 tablespoonfuls of boiling water.

Stir with a spoon until the cocoa is all dissolved and the mixture is smooth.

Put 2 cupfuls of granulated sugar into a saucepan with 1 cupful of hot water.

Stand the saucepan on a hot part of the stove and let the water come to a boil. Do not stir it.

The syrup should boil until it becomes brittle: that is until a little dropped in cold water immediately hardens and will break.

Add the cocoa and let the mixture boil until it is quite thick.

Take the pan from the stove, stir in 1 teaspoonful of vanilla, and serve hot.

This is good with ice-cream, cake, and a variety of puddings, such as snow pudding, custard, cornstarch, etc.

CUSTARD SAUCE

½ pint milk	Saucepan
1 egg	Tablespoon
Sugar	Fork
Vanilla	Bowl

Put 1 cupful of milk into a saucepan with 1 tablespoonful of granulated sugar.

Break an egg into a bowl and beat it with a fork until the white and yolk are well mixed.

Add this to the milk.

Set the saucepan on the back part of the stove or over a small flame of the chafing dish.

Let it cook until it thickens, stirring gently all the time.

Do not let it boil.

When it is quite thick, stir in a teaspoonful of vanilla, and take the pan off the stove.

This sauce is good hot or cold, on the same things as the hot chocolate sauce.

It can also be used for Floating Island, which is made by pouring this sauce over slices of stale cake and just before serving putting on top of it the beaten whites of two eggs.

CURLYLOCKS PUDDING

1 quart strawberries	Knife
1 cup sugar	Measuring cup
1 tablespoonful lemon juice	Tablespoons
	Lemon squeezer
3 tablespoonfuls cornstarch	Double boiler or chafing-dish
	Cup
	Bowls

Pick over 1 quart of strawberries or raspberries, hull them and cut them in half. It is better to wipe the berries than wash them, but sometimes they have to be washed.

Cut a lemon in half and squeeze the juice into a cup with a lemon-squeezer.

Measure 1 tablespoonful of the juice and put in the top pan of a double boiler or chafing-dish.

Add to this 1 cup of granulated sugar, and 2 cups of cold water.

Put the pan on a hot part of the stove.

Measure 3 tablespoonfuls of cornstarch, and put it in a cup half full of cold water.

Stir until the cornstarch is dissolved.

When the sugar-water has come to a hard boil, add the dissolved cornstarch gradually.

Stir until the mixture is thick and smooth.

Now set the pan onto the lower part of your chafing-dish or double boiler containing boiling water.

Put the berries into the cornstarch mixture, stir them in well and put your double boiler on a hot part of the stove.

The mixture should cook for 10 minutes.

When done, turn the pudding out into a jelly mold and put aside to cool.

Serve cold with milk or cream.

This is enough for 6 people.

When a dessert or jelly is to be served cold and turned out of a mold, the mold should be washed with very cold water before the mixture is poured in.

WAITING RULE

Make your friends wait if there's any delay,
But never your omelet, cakes or souffle,
For friends will not spoil, but the other things
　　may!

SWEET OMELET

4 eggs	Chafing-dish or double-boiler
3 teaspoonfuls powdered sugar	Teaspoon
½ teaspoonful vanilla extract	Egg-beater
	Spatula
Teaspoonful butter	2 bowls for mixing
	Fork

Take 2 eggs and separate the whites and yolks. Put the whites in one bowl and the yolks in another.

Add to the yolks 2 whole eggs, 3 generous teaspoonfuls of powdered sugar, and ½ teaspoonful vanilla. Beat with an egg-beater until very light.

Put some boiling water in the under pan of your chafing-dish or double boiler. A chafing-dish is the best, for it is easier to serve the omelet in the dish in which it is cooked, and you cannot do this with an ordinary double boiler.

Be sure that the lamp in your chafing-dish is lighted.

In the upper pan drop a teaspoonful of butter and as it melts spread it over the pan with a spoon so that the sides as well as the bottom are greased.

Whip the 2 remaining whites with an egg-beater until very stiff, and mix them with the rest of the eggs, very carefully with a fork.

Pour into the buttered pan, cover the pan and cook it without touching for 15 minutes.

Serve at once, in the same pan.

If you use a double boiler, loosen the sides of the omelet with a spatula, or flexible knife, so that it will come away from the pan, fold half of it over the other half and turn out upon a hot plate.

This is enough for 3 people.

CEREAL CAKES

Any cooked cereal	Iron sauce-pan
Tablespoonful of butter	Turning knife, or spatula
	Mixing bowl

Some day when there is cooked oatmeal, or hominy or rice, left over from breakfast, ask your mother to let you make it into a lunch dish.

Take a small iron saucepan and put it on the hot part of the stove. It should get very hot.

Take the cold cereal in your hands and mould it into little cakes about the size of fish-balls.

Put a piece of butter as big as a sugar-lump into the hot saucepan, and as soon as it is all melted, lay the little cakes into the pan.

At the end of one minute lift up one of the cakes with your turning knife and if the underside has a brown crust on it, turn the cake over.

Do the same with each cake, until all are nicely browned on both sides. They should be eaten right away, with sugar or maple syrup on them.

PAN CAKES

1 teaspoonful baking powder	Fork
1½ cups flour	1 teaspoon
2 eggs	2 mixing bowls
1 cup milk	Measuring cup
1 teaspoonful salt	Egg-beater
Butter	Flour sifter
	Saucepan
	Spatula
	Wooden spoon

Take 2 eggs and break them carefully so that the whites and yolks shall be separate, and put the yolks in one bowl, the whites in another.

Beat the whites stiff with your egg-beater, and then beat the yolks.

Sift some flour into your measuring cup until you have 1½ cupfuls.

Add 1 teaspoonful of baking powder and 1 teaspoonful of salt.

Before doing anything else, put your frying-pan on a hot part of the stove.

Sift your flour mixture into the bowl with the egg yolks, and stir them together with a wooden spoon.

Measure 1 cupful of milk, and add this to the flour and egg; stir it in a little at a time and beat the mixture well with the wooden spoon.

There must be no lumps in the batter.

Last of all mix in your beaten egg whites carefully with a fork.

Put about ½ a teaspoonful of butter into your hot pan, leaving it on the stove.

When the butter is melted pour into the pan 1 tablespoonful of the batter.

Spread this out quickly so that the batter in the pan will be very thin, and let the cake cook until it is brown on the under side.

The hotter your pan, the quicker the batter will cook, and the better your pancake will be.

You can lift up a corner to see if it is done, if you do this carefully with a spatula.

When the cake is done on one side, turn it quickly and carefully with the spatula, and brown on the other side.

Never turn a cake more than once. It spoils it.

When both sides of the cake are done, lift it out of your pan and put it on a hot plate.

Make the rest of the cakes in the same way, as rapidly as possible, and serve at once with sugar and butter, or with maple sugar or maple syrup, or with cream.

You may have to add a little butter to your pan if you find it is getting dry.

BAKING RULE

When you bake a small thing, have the oven hot,
But for baking big things, cool it off a lot.

In a too-hot oven put a pan of water,—
That will cool it nicely, or at least it oughter!

"BAKED" STEWED PEARS

Pears   Baking dish
Spices

Take some small sickle pears, wash them and put them whole into a deep dish. Sprinkle each one with a pinch of sugar, a pinch of cinnamon and a pinch of cloves.

Cover the bottom of your dish with an inch of cold water, and set in a hot oven to simmer. This usually takes 3 hours. If the water dries off, add a little more.

They are done when soft. Serve with cream or milk.

You can also use hard, green cooking pears, but these must be peeled.

BAKED POTATOES

6 potatoes   Scrubbing brush
    Fork

Choose 6 potatoes of about the same size, and scrub the dark skin well with a scrubbing brush and cold water.

Pierce them with a fork.

Put the potatoes in a hot oven and cook them with their "jackets" on for about 1 hour.

Try them with a fork in about ¾ of an hour and see if they are soft. If they are, wrap them in a clean table napkin and serve at once.

Baked potatoes are very nice with butter and salt. Some people like them with milk.

BAKED APPLES

6 apples	Apple-corer
Granulated sugar	Baking pan
Butter	Cup
Cinnamon	Fork
1 cup hot water	

Pick out 6 nice, large, cooking apples, greenings are the best; core them and put them in a pan.

Put on top of each as much granulated sugar as you can pinch between your finger and thumb, a "pinch" of cinnamon, and a bit of butter about the size of half a lump of sugar.

Pour about 1 cup of hot water into the pan, and set in a moderate oven.

It is almost impossible to say how long to leave them in!

They are done when they are soft and juicy, probably in about ½ hour.

Stick a fork into them and try them when you think they are done.

Put them in a pretty plate or bowl with all the syrup that has been cooked out of them, and serve with cream or milk.

They are nice hot or cold.

NEST EGG

Eggs	Mixing bowl
Salt	Egg-beater
Pepper	Baking bowl
	Spoon

Take a nice, fresh egg, and ask the cook to show you how to break it open carefully, and separate the white and the yolk, so that the yolk will not be broken. Leave the yolk in a half egg-shell, and let the white fall into a mixing bowl.

Add a pinch of salt to the white, and beat with an egg-beater until it is very stiff.

Have ready some little bowl or deep saucer that is pretty enough to put on the table, and yet will not break in the oven.

Into this dish pour the stiff-beaten white, and make a little hole in the middle of the white with a spoon.

In this little hollow place put the yolk, still unbroken.

Set the dish in a hot oven and cook for two or three minutes, or until the white is a little brown and the yolk is firm.

Serve right away.

There must be a separate dish for each egg.

TAPIOCA PUDDING

3 tablespoonfuls pearl tapioca	Mixing bowls
1 quart milk	Tablespoon
2 tablespoonfuls sugar	Teaspoon
1 egg	Baking dish
2 teaspoonfuls vanilla	Egg-beater

Put 3 tablespoonfuls of pearl tapioca into half a cup of cold water and leave it for half an hour or more.

Break an egg into a mixing bowl and beat with an egg-beater until it is very light.

Add to this 2 tablespoonfuls of granulated sugar and 2 teaspoonfuls of vanilla extract, and mix them all together.

Pour over this 1 quart of milk and mix well.

Strain the water from the tapioca and add the tapioca to the mixture, and pour the whole into a pretty baking dish of some sort.

Bake for one hour in a moderate oven.

Serve cold in the same dish, with sugar and cream or milk.

This is enough for six people.

SPOONFULS AND CUPFULS

Fill to a level spoon or cup,
Unless you're *told* to heap it up.

SCALLOPED FISH

Cold fish   Saucepan
Butter   Fork
Flour   Spoons
Milk   Baking dish
Pepper
Salt
Bread crumbs

Take some cold fish, say enough to make 1 pint, and pick it to pieces with a silver fork. Be sure to take out every bone.

Make a cream sauce, as you have learned to do, with 1 tablespoonful of flour, 1 tablespoonful of butter and 1 cup of milk. Use a saucepan or double boiler and be careful not to let it burn.

Add 1 teaspoonful of salt and a little pepper.

Put your fish into the saucepan with the sauce, mix it all up well, and take from the stove.

Take a baking dish and butter the sides and bottom carefully.

Turn the fish into the baking dish.

Have ready about ½ a cup of stale bread crumbs, add to them a pinch of salt and a smaller pinch of pepper, mix them all up, and sprinkle over the fish.

Drop some very small bits of butter on the top

and put the dish in a pretty hot oven to brown. This should take about fifteen minutes, but it might take less or more according to the heat of the oven.

Take the fish out when the top is brown, and serve right away.

This can be baked in little dishes or in large shells.

RICE PUDDING

4 tablespoons rice Mixing bowl
4 tablespoons sugar Strainer or sieve
Nutmeg Enamel baking dish
1 quart milk

Take 4 tablespoonfuls of rice, pick out all the specks and dried kernels and wash it by putting it in a strainer or sieve and letting clean, cold water run over it.

Put the washed rice into a bowl, and add 4 tablespoonfuls of granulated sugar.

Pour over the rice 1 quart of good milk.

Turn the mixture into a baking dish. The pudding will be creamier if you use an enameled metal one, but you can use china.

Grate over the top some nutmeg, and set the dish in a moderate oven.

Cook for about 2 hours. From time to time as the pudding begins to get brown on top, stir down the top crust. Do this twice. When the rice is thoroughly soft it is done.

Rice pudding is better served quite cold.

If you like raisins, get some of the seedless kind, measure about 2 tablespoonfuls and soak them in boiling water for 5 minutes. Drain off the water and stir them into the pudding before you put it into the oven.

THE STRAW TEST

With a straw I pierce my cake,
When I think it's cooked enough.
If the straw gets sticky rough,
I must longer bake.
If it come out clean and neat,
Then the cake is fit to eat.

CUP CUSTARD FOR THREE

2 eggs	Egg-beater
Granulated sugar	Saucepan
Salt	Grater
Nutmeg	Baking dishes
Hot water	Baking pan
1 pint milk	Mixing bowl
	Spoon

Break 2 eggs carefully into a bowl and beat with an egg-beater for three minutes.

Add ¼ teaspoonful salt and 2 heaping tablespoonfuls of granulated sugar. Beat with a spoon for two minutes.

Heat 1 pint of milk in a saucepan until it is very hot, but not boiling, and mix with the egg and sugar, beating it again for a minute with your spoon.

Take 3 small dishes or 1 large one, that will be pretty and yet stand baking, and pour the mixture in.

Grate a little nutmeg over the top.

Put the baking dishes into a pan, and put the pan into a moderately hot oven. Before you shut the oven door pour some hot water into the pan, carefully, so that none of it will get into the custards; the water should come up about half-way to the top of the custard cups.

Cook until the custards are firm in the middle and brown on top. If you use the little cups or dishes this should take about half an hour. The larger dish will take longer.

Use the straw test.

Take them out of the pan and set them where they will cool. Serve them very cold.

If you have no pretty dish, fold a clean table napkin so that it will be the width of the dish, lay it around the dish and pin it together.

CHICKEN CUSTARD

1 cup thick chicken stock	Measuring cup
	Custard cups
1 cup cream or milk	Double boiler
Yolks of 3 eggs	Egg-beater
1 teaspoonful salt	Teaspoon
	Bowl

Some day when the cook has some good, rich chicken stock in the house, measure out 1 cupful and put it in the top part of a double boiler.

Add to it 1 cup of cream, or if you have no cream, 1 cupful of milk into which you have stirred 1 teaspoonful of melted butter. The cream or milk must be absolutely fresh or your custard will curdle.

Put your pan on the stove and cook your milk and stock until it begins to smoke.

Do not let it come to a boil.

While this is cooking, break open 3 eggs carefully, and separate the whites and yolks.

The whites can be put away in the ice-box for future use.

Beat the yolks with an egg-beater until they are stiff.

When your milk and chicken is ready, take it

from the stove and add the beaten egg-yolks and 1 teaspoonful of salt.

Mix well with a spoon.

Put the pan into the double boiler and set it on a hot part of the stove.

Cook until the mixture begins to get thick.

Pour it into custard cups and set in a cold place to get hard and cold.

Serve cold.

This ought to be enough for 5 people.

It is nice for a hearty supper or lunch dish, also to serve to invalids.

BROWN BETTY

6 cooking apples	Apple corer
½ cup molasses	Measuring cup
½ cup cold water	Baking dish
4 tablespoonfuls brown sugar	Knife
Butter	
Bread crumbs	

Take 6 large, tart apples, core them and peel them and cut them into small slices.

Take a baking dish, butter the inside and cover the bottom with one layer of apple slices.

Sprinkle a layer of bread crumbs over the apple, then lay more apple over the crumbs, and so on until you have used all the apple.

There must be crumbs on top.

Measure ½ cupful of black molasses and ½ cupful of cold water.

Add to this 4 tablespoonfuls of brown sugar, and stir until the sugar is dissolved.

Pour the mixture over the apple and crumbs, and drop four little bits of butter on top of all.

Put the dish in a moderate oven for about ¾ of an hour, or until it is nicely browned on top, and the apples are soft. Try them with a fork.

Serve hot with cream or a hard sauce.

WETS AND DRYS

Have one bowl for liquids,
Put drys in another;
And just before cooking
Mix all up together.

MEAT LOAF

1 pound chopped raw beef	Rolling pin and board
4 white crackers	Mixing bowl
½ cup cream or milk (or some evaporated cream)	Wooden spoon
	Teaspoon
	Measuring cup
	Baking dish
1 egg	
1 teaspoonful salt	
Butter	

Take 4 white crackers,—any simple unsweetened cracker will do.

Roll them into fine crumbs with your rolling pin.

Put them in a bowl with 1 teaspoonful of salt.

(Leave out some of the crumbs to put on top of your loaf.)

Break an egg into the bowl and mix well with the cracker crumbs, using a wooden spoon.

Put into the bowl 1 pound of finely chopped raw beef, and mix again.

Measure ½ cup of cream and pour over the mixture. (You can use instead 4 tablespoonfuls of unsweetened evaporated cream.) If you use milk, add to it 1 tablespoonful of melted butter before you pour it on the meat.

Mix the whole together again, and turn into your baking dish, moulding it into a loaf with a spoon.

Sprinkle over the top the rest of your cracker crumbs, and a tablespoonful of butter broken into little pieces.

Bake in a moderate oven for about 25 minutes, until the meat is nicely browned on top.

Serve hot or cold, if possible in the dish in which the loaf was cooked.

BIRTHDAY CAKE

2 heaping tablespoonfuls butter	3 mixing bowls
	Wooden spoon
	Measuring cup
6 heaping tablespoonfuls sugar	Tablespoon
	Teaspoon
	Egg-beater
½ cup milk	Baking pan
1½ cups flour	Flour sifter
½ lemon	Lemon squeezer
2 eggs	Knife
2 teaspoonfuls baking powder	

Take 2 eggs, break them carefully, and put the whites in one bowl and the yolks in another. Beat the whites first, so as not to soil your beater and then beat the yolks.

Put 6 heaping tablespoonfuls of granulated sugar in a third bowl, add to this 2 heaping tablespoonfuls of butter, which has been softened by warming it on the stove.

Beat the butter and sugar together with a wooden spoon until they are well mixed and light.

Add the yolks of the eggs and beat again for 5 minutes. Add ½ teaspoonful of salt.

Sift some flour and measure 1½ cupfuls into the empty bowl. Have ready ½ cup of milk.

Cut a lemon in half and squeeze one-half carefully, through a squeezer, on the sugar and egg and butter. Mix them together with a spoon.

Now add your flour and milk a little at a time and beat the whole until it is quite smooth and free from lumps.

Before doing anything more examine your oven and if you want to make a loaf cake have a moderate oven. If you are going to make little cakes you will want a hot one.

Butter your tins well, using either a big tin for loaf cake or a muffin tin for little ones.

Measure 2 teaspoonfuls of baking powder and add them to the dough. Last of all add the beaten whites of the eggs, mix them in with a fork, and turn the dough at once into the buttered tin.

Never let cake dough stand after the baking powder is in it.

If you bake it in one loaf it will take about ¾ of an hour.

Twenty minutes is generally right for small cakes.

Use the straw test when you think your cake

is done, but do not keep opening the oven door. Do not open it at all for some time after the cake is in.

When it is done turn out onto a plate to cool.

OVEN DOORS

Never slam the oven door,—
Cakes will fall to rise no more.

HILDA'S JOHNNY CAKE

1 egg	Measuring cup
1 cup flour	Teaspoon
1/3 cup cornmeal	Baking tin
1/4 cup sugar	Egg-beater
2 teaspoonfuls baking powder	Mixing bowl
	Tablespoon
1/2 teaspoonful salt	Flour sifter
1 tablespoonful melted butter	
3/4 cup milk	
Butter or lard for greasing pan	

Measure 1 cupful of white flour and 1/3 of a cup of yellow cornmeal.

Be sure your flour and meal are sifted before you measure them.

Add 1/4 cup of granulated sugar, 2 teaspoonfuls of baking powder and 1/2 teaspoonful of salt.

Mix them up well with a spoon, or sift them once more all together.

Get your baking tin and grease it carefully. Be sure that your oven is all right.

Break an egg into a bowl and beat it with an egg-beater.

Mix it in with the dry things.

Then add about ¾ cup of milk, and 1 tablespoonful of melted butter.

You may need more milk, you may need less. You want enough to moisten the flour so that it will form a dough that you can drop into the pan.

Mix the milk in as fast as you can, but thoroughly, so that your dough will be smooth.

Pour into the buttered tin and bake in a moderate oven.

It is better to have a shallow pan; your dough should be only about 1 inch thick before it is cooked.

Bake it about 20 minutes or until it is brown.

Use straw test.

Do not open the oven door for at least ten minutes after your pan is in the oven.

BLUEBERRY MUFFINS

½ cupful sugar
1 egg
½ cupful milk
Teaspoonful baking powder
1 tablespoonful butter
1 cupful flour
1 cupful blueberries
½ teaspoonful salt

Measuring cup
2 mixing bowls
Wooden spoon
Teaspoon
Tablespoon
Muffin tin
Flour sifter

Put ½ cupful of granulated sugar into a bowl.

Break 2 eggs into the bowl and beat the sugar and eggs together with a wooden spoon.

Melt 1 tablespoonful of butter on the stove and mix it in with the eggs and sugar.

Sift some flour into your measuring cup until you have 1 cupful.

Add to this ½ teaspoonful of salt and 1 teaspoonful of baking powder.

Sift together into the bowl with the eggs and sugar and butter.

See that your oven is hot and butter your muffin tins.

Measure 1 cupful of blueberries, put them in a bowl, and pick them over; wash them if necessary, but it is better only to wipe them with a cloth.

Measure ½ cup of milk and add this gradually to the flour mixture. Beat it with your wooden spoon as you mix in the milk.

When you have beaten the mixture so that it is smooth and light, put in the cupful of blueberries, and mix it all together thoroughly.

Pour into your buttered tins, filling them half full.

Bake in a quick oven for about 15 minutes.

Use the straw test. Do not open the oven door for at least ten minutes after your muffins are in the oven.

When the muffins are done, turn them out on a plate.

KATY'S GINGERBREAD

1 egg	Teaspoon
½ cup brown sugar	Tablespoon
2 tablespoonfuls butter	Wooden stirring spoon
	Measuring cup
Bacon fat	Two mixing bowls
1 cup black molasses	Egg-beater
2 cups flour	Flour sifter
½ teaspoonful salt	Saucepan
1 teaspoonful cinnamon	Baking pan
	Spatula
½ teaspoonful allspice	
½ teaspoonful ginger	
1 cup boiling water	
1 teaspoonful cooking soda	

Take a fresh egg and break it carefully into a large bowl. Beat it with an egg-beater until it is very stiff.

Pour half a cupful of brown sugar into the egg and mix well.

Put 2 tablespoonfuls of butter and some bacon fat into a pan and melt them together on the stove. Use enough bacon-fat to give you, with the butter, a half-cupful of melted grease.

Stir this in with the sugar and egg.

Before you do anything more, be sure that the oven is hot, and that you have ready a good-sized shallow baking-pan, smeared on the inside with butter.

Put a cup of black molasses into the mixture and beat for two minutes with a wooden spoon.

Take another bowl and sift into it with a flour-sifter 2 cups of flour, ½ teaspoonful of salt, one heaping teaspoonful of cinnamon, ½ teaspoonful of allspice, and ½ teaspoonful of ginger; stir this slowly into the mixture in the first bowl, and beat for three minutes, if it is not thick and stiff, sift a little more flour, perhaps ¼ of a cup, and add it, mixing well.

Dissolve a teaspoonful of cooking soda in a cup of boiling water, put this quickly into the other mixture and beat again for three minutes.

Now pour it all into your buttered pan, and set it carefully into the hot oven. Don't leave the oven door open longer than you can help.

Bake for about 12 minutes and use the straw test to see if it is done.

Gingerbread should be carefully loosened from the pan with a flexible knife, called a spatula, and turned on a big plate to cool. Do not cut it, but break it.

GINGERBREAD PUDDING

Bake some gingerbread according to the preceding receipt, but use a small deep tin so that you will have a thick loaf. Serve this fresh and hot, with a vanilla sauce. The sauce is made as follows:

VANILLA SAUCE

Break an egg into a bowl.

Beat it hard with an egg-beater.

Stir into it ½ pint of milk and one tablespoonful of sugar.

Put into a sauce-pan and cook over a slow fire, stirring all the time in the same direction.

Take it off when it begins to thicken and before it comes to a boil.

Add 7 drops of vanilla and stir well.

Serve it hot with the gingerbread.

SIFTING AND STIRRING

Sift your flour before you measure.
A wooden stirring spoon's a treasure.

TEA-PARTY BISCUIT

1 cup flour	Flour sifter
1 teaspoonful baking powder	Measuring cup
	Wooden spoon
½ cup milk or water	Teaspoons
¼ teaspoonful salt	Mixing bowl
4 teaspoonfuls butter or lard	Flour board and rolling pin
	Biscuit cutter
	Baking tin
	Spatula

Sift some flour into a cup until it is full.

Add to this 1 teaspoonful of baking powder and ¼ of a teaspoonful of salt. Sift again together into a bowl.

Take 4 teaspoonfuls of butter or lard and rub it into your flour with your fingers. There must be no lumps of butter left but the whole mixture should be dry and crumbly.

Butter a shallow baking tin.

Get out your flour board and sift a little flour on it. This is to prevent your dough sticking to the board when you roll it out.

Sift some on the rolling pin, too.

After everything is ready, add your ½ cup of milk to the flour, and mix it in quickly with a spoon.

Turn the soft dough onto your board and roll it out with the rolling pin. Always roll the dough away from you.

Roll it very lightly, without pressing hard on the rolling pin.

When you have a sheet of dough about ½ inch thick, cut out round pieces with a cutter. Use one about as large as a napkin-ring.

Do this quickly.

With a spatula lift the round pieces, carefully so as not to break them, and lay them on the buttered tin. They must not quite touch each other.

Bake in a fairly hot oven for 15 minutes.

The biscuit must be brown on top and about 1 and ½ inches high when done.

SATURDAY COOKIES

3 tablespoonfuls butter	Saucepan
¾ cup sugar	Measuring cup
6 teaspoonfuls rich milk	Tablespoon and teaspoon
¼ teaspoonful soda	Wooden spoon
¼ teaspoonful salt	Spatula
½ teaspoonful vanilla	Mixing bowls
1 egg	Shallow baking tins
1½ cups flour	Flour sifter
	Flour board and rolling pin
	Cooky cutter
	Egg-beater

Measure 3 tablespoonfuls of butter and put in a saucepan on the stove to melt.

Put ¾ of a cup of granulated sugar in a mixing bowl, and add the melted butter, rubbing them together well with a wooden spoon.

Add to this ½ teaspoonful of vanilla extract.

Break an egg into another bowl and beat it with an egg beater until it is quite light.

Add this to the butter and sugar, and beat together with a spoon.

Before doing anything more, get your board and rolling pin ready, and butter your baking tins. See that your oven is hot.

Dissolve ¼ of a teaspoonful of cooking soda in a tablespoonful of hot water.

Sift some flour and measure 1½ cupfuls into a bowl. Sift this again with ¼ of a teaspoonful of salt.

Add 6 teaspoonfuls of rich milk to your soda water and add this to your first mixture, at the same time adding the flour.

Mix it well as you put in the flour and milk, so that your dough may not be lumpy.

Sift a little flour onto your board and rolling pin so that the dough will not stick to either, and turn the dough onto the board.

Roll it out with the rolling pin, until it is very thin, less than ½ an inch.

Always roll away from yourself.

Now cut the thin sheet of dough with a cooky cutter, and when it is all cut, lift the pieces carefully with a spatula and put them on the buttered tins, so that they will not touch each other.

Bake in a hot oven for about 15 minutes. They should get a little brown. Use the straw test.

Turn the cookies onto a plate to cool.

JUNKET

1 quart milk	Mixing bowl
2 tablespoonfuls powdered sugar	Tablespoon
	Teaspoon
1 teaspoonful vanilla extract	
1 tablespoonful liquid rennet	

Put a quart of milk into a mixing bowl and stir into it 2 tablespoonfuls of powdered sugar and 1 teaspoonful of vanilla extract.

Measure 1 tablespoonful from a bottle of liquid rennet, which can generally be bought at a drug store, or any large grocery store.

Add this to the milk, stir it well, and pour the whole into little glasses or into cups or a glass bowl.

Set this in a warm room until the milk has become firm, like custard.

Then put it in the ice chest until you are ready to eat it.

In summer do not make it more than 2 hours before you are going to eat it.

It can be served with sugar and cream, or with any cold fruit or chocolate sauce.

This makes enough for 5 people.

BREAD-AND-BUTTER RULE

Butter your bread before you slice
If you want your sandwich nice.

SCHOOL SANDWICHES

To make good sandwiches it is necessary to have bread that is at least a day old, a sharp knife, and soft butter. Soften your butter by putting it in a dish at the back of the stove for a few minutes.

Butter your loaf of bread before cutting off each slice and cut the slices thin. Lay the buttered slices neatly together and trim off the crusts. Various fillings can be used; any kind of cold meat, chopped up fine, cheese, jam, jelly, or slices of hard boiled egg.

You can make a most delicious sandwich out of thin slices of brown bread, with a filling of the cottage cheese on page 67. Cottage cheese mixed with a little jam is a delicious filling for white bread sandwiches.

A slice of plain cake and a slice of buttered bread together make a very good combination.

FAIRY SALAD

1 head lettuce	Dish pan
Sugar	Sharp knife
1 orange	Cloth

Choose a nice head of lettuce, one that has no faded leaves and that seems solid.

Carefully pull the leaves from the stem, so that the tender white ends will come off too.

Cut off the flat white root if it is headed lettuce. Most people do not like it.

Throw away any tough or faded leaves and put the tender fresh leaves into a dish pan filled with cold water.

Leave the lettuce in this for half an hour or more, then take it out, and shake off the water carefully. Sometimes you may need to use a cloth to dry the leaves.

Take an orange, slice it with a sharp knife and cut off the skin. Try not to lose any juice.

Put the lettuce leaves into a dish, lay the orange slices on them, and sprinkle the whole with ½ a cup of granulated sugar.

Put the bowl in the ice closet for a short time, and serve very soon.

If you have a big orange it is better to cut the slices in small pieces.

LEMONADE

2 lemons	Lemon squeezer
10 teaspoonfuls granulated sugar	Measuring cup
	Teaspoon
4 cupfuls water	Pitcher
	Knife

Cut two lemons in half and squeeze the juice into a pitcher with a lemon squeezer.

Add to this 10 teaspoonfuls of granulated sugar, and stir it until the sugar is dissolved.

Add 4 cupfuls of cold water and mix it well.

This will make 4 glasses of plain lemonade. If you want more, add the juice of ½ lemon, 2 teaspoonfuls sugar and 1 cup water for each glass.

It is very nice to add to the lemonade any fruit or berries in season.

Cut bananas or oranges or peaches, etc., into slices. Berries should be crushed with a little sugar.

Ps AND Qs

Two cupfuls make a pint; in short
Four even cupfuls make a quart.
And folks have found this saying sound—
A pint's a pound the world around.

COTTAGE CHEESE

Pint or more of sour milk	Glass milk bottle or pitcher
Salt	Mixing bowl
Tablespoonful fresh milk	Half-yard of white cheese-cloth

If your mother will let you have some sour milk or cream, it is very easy to make cottage cheese.

Put the sour milk into a glass milk bottle, or pitcher, and let it stand in a warm room, until it begins to curd; that is, until the thick part is very thick and lumpy, and there is a little thin liquid at the bottom.

This may take twelve hours, or it may take as much as two days.

Then stand the bottle at the back of the stove, to heat slowly for fifteen or twenty minutes, until the thick part and the liquid are entirely separate.

Now take a piece of white cheese-cloth, as big as a table napkin, lay this over a bowl, and pour the whole mixture into the cloth.

Gather up the corners of the cheese-cloth and tie them together, making a sort of loose bag. Let this hang suspended over the bowl for twenty-four hours, thus allowing the thin liquid to drip away, and the cheese to dry.

The water in the bowl can be thrown away, or given to the dog. It is good for him.

Take the firm ball of cheese out of its bag, put it in a dish, and just before you want to serve it, soften it by mixing into it a tablespoonful of fresh milk into which you have put a pinch of salt.

This ought to be nicer cheese than you can buy at any store, and is very good eaten with jam and bread-and-butter.

CLAM BROTH

1 pint soft clams
Salt
Pepper
1 tablespoonful butter
Cold water

A large soup pot
Strainer
Bowl

Put 1 pint of fresh soft clams into a large pot and pour enough cold water over them to cover them.

Stand the pot on a hot part of the stove until the water boils up hard.

Take the pot off and strain the water and juice through a fine strainer into a bowl.

The clams are very nice to eat just as they are, with salt and pepper and butter, but if you do not care for them they can be given to the cat or dog, who will probably appreciate them.

Put into the broth 1 teaspoonful of salt and ¼ of a teaspoonful of pepper and 1 tablespoonful of butter.

Put it back into the pot and stand on the stove to get really hot again but do not let it boil up.

Serve hot.

This makes enough broth for 8 people.

SIMMERING RULE

Put your soup meat in a pot
Where the stove is not too hot;
Boiling slow with moderate heat
Draws the juices from the meat.

BEEF TEA

1 pound beef	Saucepan
1 pint cold water	Cheese cloth
Salt and pepper	

Take 1 pound of beef, either from the neck or round where the meat is tough, but juicy and cheap; have the butcher or the cook chop it up for you.

Put it in a saucepan and pour over it 1 pint of cold water.

Let it stand for one hour to soak.

Put the pan at the back of the stove and let the meat cook until it is steaming hot.

Stir in 2 teaspoonfuls of salt and ½ teaspoonful of pepper.

Strain the meat through a piece of cheese-cloth and let the soup pass into a serving dish or cup and serve at once.

This makes 2 cups of broth.

MILK TOAST

Bread	Toaster or toasting fork
Butter	
2 cupfuls milk	Saucepan
Salt and pepper	Measuring cup
	Knife

First make your toast; this is best done over a hot fire, with a toaster, but you can make quite good toast in the oven.

Cut enough thin slices of bread for your guests, allowing about two a piece. Stale bread is better than fresh.

Lay these slices on a toaster, if you have one, or hold them one at a time on a long fork.

Take off one of the stove covers and toast your bread over a hot fire until one side is brown, and then toast it on the other side.

Be sure not to burn it.

If you use the oven, lay the bread in a pan.

If the fire is not hot the toast will be tough and hard. This is generally the trouble when toast is made in the oven, or when it is made before you want to use it.

Butter your toast evenly, and lay it in a hot dish.

Sprinkle a pinch of salt and one of pepper over each piece.

Heat 2 cupfuls of milk in a saucepan, until it steams.

Pour the hot milk over the toast and serve **at** once in the same dish.

If you use more than 8 pieces of toast you will need more milk.

Cream toast can be made by using the sauce described on page 7 instead of the hot milk. In this case don't put the salt and pepper on the toast.

RULE FOR SERVING COLD

Jellies and dishes you want cold and nice,
Must first be cooled slowly and then put on ice
For six hours, or more, if you take my advice.

BLACKBERRY BREAD

1 loaf stale bread	Sharp bread knife
Butter	Broad knife
1 quart blackberries	Saucepan
Sugar	Spoon
¾ cup cold water	

Take a loaf of stale bread, butter one end, and cut off a thin slice. The bread must be quite stale. Continue to butter and slice until you have used the whole loaf. It is always easier and nicer to butter your bread before slicing.

Put 1 quart of blackberries in a saucepan with about 1 cupful of granulated sugar and ¾ cup of cold water. Simmer the berries until they are tender, and the juice is running freely.

This will probably take about fifteen minutes. Stir from time to time. Put a layer of buttered bread into a deep dish and pour some of the hot stewed berries over it, then more bread and more blackberries in layers until all are used.

Put the dish in a cold place until the berries have cooled and then set on ice for a while.

Serve in the same dish with cream or milk.

Strawberry, raspberry or cherry bread can be made in the same way. Use more sugar with the sour berries, less with sweet.

ANGEL HASH

2 oranges	Sharp vegetable knife
2 bananas	Mixing spoon
1 cup sugar	Measuring cup
½ lemon	Lemon squeezer

Take 2 fine juicy oranges and cut them, without peeling, into thin slices, across the grain.

Cut them carefully over some dish, with a sharp knife, so as not to lose any of the juice.

Trim the hard outside skin away and lay the slices in a pretty glass or china bowl. If you have any juice that spilled while you were cutting the oranges, pour this in too.

Sprinkle ½ cup sugar over the oranges.

Take 2 firm bananas, peel off the skin, and cut the fruit into slices about as thick as your finger, and lay them on top of the orange slices. If you have any apples or other fruit, it is nice to add some slices, but be sure to peel and stone the fruit, and never let any seeds drop into the dish.

Squeeze ½ lemon into the dish, and sprinkle over the whole another ½ cup of sugar.

Leave the dish in a moderately warm room for 2 hours, then mix up the fruit with a spoon, and put it on ice. Serve in the same dish.

This is enough for three.

JELLY WHIP

Whites of 3 eggs Mixing bowl
3 tablespoonfuls Tablespoon
  powdered sugar Teaspoon
½ cup currant jelly

Separate carefully the whites and yolks of 3 eggs. Put the yolks away in a cup for some future use.

Put the whites in a bowl and beat with an egg-beater until very stiff and light.

Get some currant, or raspberry, or strawberry jelly, and measure about ½ cupful. Add this to the egg-whites, one teaspoonful at a time, beating the mixture between each additional teaspoonful of jelly.

When all the jelly is mixed with the egg, beat it a few minutes more for good luck, and to make sure that it is all light and fluffy.

Heap it in a dish or into small glasses and serve it right away.

This should be more than enough for three people.

Be careful, when putting in the jelly, to add a very little at a time, or it will make the egg heavy, so that you cannot beat it.

MOCK WINE JELLY

½ cupful prune syrup	Measuring cup
¼ box gelatine	1 cup
1 banana	1 bowl
1 orange	Jelly mold
1 cup sugar	Knife
1 lemon	Wooden spoon
	Lemon squeezer
	Cheese-cloth

Put ¼ of a box of gelatine into a cup holding ½ a pint of cold water and let it soak for ½ an hour.

Take ½ cup of prune syrup from some stewed prunes (the receipt for stewing prunes is given under stewed fruits) and put it in a bowl.

Peel and slice a banana and put the slices in the bowl.

Peel and slice an orange and add that too.

Measure 1 cup of granulated sugar and add that.

Squeeze the juice of one lemon over the fruit.

When your gelatine has soaked for ½ an hour strain into the bowl through 2 thicknesses of cheese-cloth and pour over the whole 1 cup of boiling water.

Put the bowl in a cold place and stir the mixture well with a spoon.

When it is quite cold beat it hard for a few minutes with your spoon.

Pour the mixture into a cold jelly mold, and let it stand on ice until it is stiff. This will take a number of hours.

This is enough for 4 people.

BOILING RULE

Boil your water hard to brew
Tea that's good, and cocoa too.
Tea itself should not be boiled;
Boil your cocoa or it's spoiled!

WAYS TO MAKE GOOD TEA

In order to make good tea you must use water that is really boiling hard.

First heat your tea-pot by pouring some hot water into it.

Empty it and put in your tea, 1 teaspoonful for each cup.

If you want to make four cups of tea, pour 1 cup of boiling water into the pot onto your tea and let it stand for 3 minutes. Then add the other 3 cups of boiling water and let it stand for 1 minute.

Serve at once with sugar and cream, or sugar and slices of lemon.

Never let tea stand on the tea grounds. If you are not ready to drink the tea when it is done, pour it into another pot or pitcher through a strainer.

You can make very good tea by using a tea-ball. Put your tea into the tea-ball and put the tea-ball into the individual cups; pour the boiling water over and when the tea is strong enough remove the tea-ball. This has the advantage of never letting the tea stand on the leaves or grounds.

If you want to make a great quantity of tea,

for a reception or party, a very good thing to do is to make a number of little cheese-cloth bags and fill them with tea. These can be put into your tea-pot and when the tea is strong enough can be removed, in that way keeping the tea fresh during a long period of time.

It is also possible to make a very thick tea syrup, by pouring a small quantity of boiling water over a large quantity of tea, and after it has stood for 3 minutes pouring it off into a tea-pot. This will keep for a day and can be diluted with hot water whenever a cup of tea is wanted. Put a small quantity in the cup, and pour as much hot water over it as is needed. This water does not need to be boiling, only hot, as the tea itself was made with boiling water.

HOW TO MAKE ONE CUP OF COCOA

1 teaspoonful cocoa
1 tablespoonful boiling water
½ pint milk
1 teaspoonful granulated sugar

Tablespoon
Measuring cup
Saucepan

Take a teaspoonful of cocoa, and put it in a tin cup.

Add 1 teaspoonful of granulated sugar and one tablespoonful boiling water from the kettle.

Mix it well so that there will not be any lumps of cocoa.

Pour a little less than ½ pint of milk into a saucepan and cook it, stirring all the time until it is scalded; that is, until a film forms on it and it just begins to bubble.

Stir the cocoa mixture into this, and cook it until it boils up.

It burns very easily, so stir it carefully.

Pour into a large cup and serve. To keep the cup from cracking, put a teaspoon in it before you pour in the hot cocoa.

CANDY RULE

When you make candy, no matter what's in it,
Watch it with care for it spoils in a minute.

POPPITY CORN

Ears of popcorn Deep saucepan with
A little oil or butter cover
  or lard

Ordinary popcorn is made with a corn-popper. Poppity Corn is made in a deep covered dish on the stove, and is much fluffier and lighter.

The most important thing is to have fresh popcorn. Old corn is hard and small after it is popped. It is always best to get popcorn on the ear and shell it yourself.

Take the deep saucepan and put two or three tablespoonfuls of salad oil, or butter or lard in it, and ½ teaspoonful of salt. The bottom should be barely covered.

Put the dish on a hot part of the stove, and when the oil is very hot indeed throw in a handful of popcorn, and put the cover on.

While the corn is popping you may shake the dish a little, but it does not need to be shaken hard. When the corn is all popped the oil will be gone, and you can empty the corn onto a plate.

A bowl of popcorn and milk is very good.

A bowl of popcorn with a little melted butter stirred into it is a dish that many people like.

POPCORN BALLS

Have a bowl of popped corn all ready.

Put in a saucepan half a cupful of granulated sugar and 4 tablespoonfuls of water, and place on a hot part of the stove. Boil this until you have a thick syrup that will be hard when tested in cold water.

Put the pan at the back of the stove where the syrup will keep hot but not boil anymore. Pick up pieces of popcorn, one by one, and dip them into the syrup and stick them together, adding more and more of them until you have made a ball. Let these harden in a cold place.

POPCORN PATTIES

Boil together 1 cup of sugar and ½ cupful of molasses, until it is thick and waxy when a few drops are tested in cold water.

Stir into this a quart of popped corn. Have ready a cold buttered plate.

Spoon up heaping spoonfuls of the mixture and drop them in little patties onto the plate. Set in a cold place to harden.

CANDIED ORANGE-PEEL

Peel of 6 oranges	Bowl
2½ cups granulated sugar	Saucepan
	Spoon
Water	Fork
1 teaspoonful salt	Sharp knife

Put about 1 quart of cold water into a bowl and add to it 1 teaspoonful of salt.

Keep the bowl of water in a cold place and put into it orange peelings as you get them. It is all right to use what is left from the table.

Scrape off all of the pulp and most of the inner white skin with a sharp knife.

Leave the peel in the salt water for a few days, adding more peel. When you have the peel from about 6 oranges, pour off the salt water and wash the peel with fresh water so that any salt taste may be washed away. Cut the peel into short narrow strips, about 2 or 3 inches long and as wide as your little finger.

Put the peel into a saucepan and pour over it 1 quart of cold water.

Set the saucepan on a hot part of the stove and cook the peel until it is soft. This may take an hour or more.

Try it with a fork to see if it is done, and when

it is, take the pan from the stove. Add to the water and peel about 1 pint more cold water, or enough to have a quart of water altogether, with what is left in the saucepan, and put 2 cups of granulated sugar in with it.

Set the pan on the stove again and let the water and sugar cook until the water has nearly boiled away, leaving the peel covered with a thick syrup.

This will take some time.

Take the pan off the stove.

Put some granulated sugar on a plate and drop the orange peel, piece by piece, into the sugar and roll it with a fork so that it will be well coated.

When the peel is cold it is ready to eat.

RAINY-DAY FUDGE

2 cups granulated sugar	Measuring cup
1 cup milk	Chafing-dish or saucepan
Butter	Knife
Teaspoonful vanilla	Stirring spoon
¼ pound chocolate, or 4 heaping tablespoons cocoa	Teaspoon
	Glass of cold water
	Greased paper or pan

Measure 2 cups of granulated sugar and put it in a saucepan with 1 cup of milk. Add a lump of butter about the size of a lump of sugar.

Put the pan on a hot part of the stove, and while the milk is heating, cut up ¼ pound of chocolate into little pieces.

If you use cocoa, put 4 heaping tablespoonfuls right in with the milk, without waiting. Chocolate and cocoa must both be unsweetened.

When the milk and sugar in the pan begin to get smoking hot, add your chocolate.

Cook for 15 or 20 minutes, stirring all the time.

Be sure that the pan is on a hot part of the stove and that you stir it well so that it will not burn.

When you think it's done, try it and see. **Dip**

a little out with a teaspoon and drop it in a glass of cold water. If it gets thick and stiff, you may be sure the rest is done.

Take the pan off the stove, add 1 teaspoonful of vanilla extract and beat it together with a spoon for three minutes.

Take your greased paper and lay it on a plate, or better still, take the baking tin which you have smeared with butter, and pour over it the hot fudge.

Leave the fudge in a cold place to harden.

When it is perfectly firm, cut it into squares with a sharp knife.

It should be about ½ an inch thick, so do not try to fill too large a pan.

It is not always necessary to cook fudge for 20 minutes, so it is just as well to try it after 10 or 15 minutes.

This receipt makes nearly a pound of candy.

MOLASSES CANDY

1 cupful molasses	Measuring cup
1 cupful brown sugar	Tablespoon
1 tablespoonful vinegar	Saucepan
	Pans
2 tablespoonfuls butter	Glass or cup

Take a large saucepan and put into it 1 cupful of molasses, 1 cupful of brown sugar, 1 tablespoonful of vinegar, and 2 tablespoonfuls of butter.

Set the saucepan on a hot part of the stove and when the mixture boils, look at the clock and let it boil for about 15 minutes.

Test a spoonful of it in a glass of cold water. If the mixture becomes hard and breakable at once, it is done. It should be much harder than the peppermint syrup.

Rub a shallow baking tin with butter and into this pour the mixture at once.

Put the pan in a cool place.

As soon as the mixture is cold enough to touch without burning your fingers, spoon out pieces as big as your fist and have each person take one of the pieces.

Pull it apart with your two hands and twist it,

and pull it, until it gets a nice light yellow and is so stiff that you can't pull it any more.

Twist it into long thin ropes and let them get entirely hard on buttered plates in the ice chest. Then break into short pieces for eating.

This makes enough for four children to pull.

It is very important to have your hands clean before you begin pulling the candy.

PEPPERMINT DROPS FOR TWO CHILDREN TO MAKE

2 cupfuls sugar   Measuring cup
1 cupful water   Saucepan
1 teaspoonful extract   Teaspoon
   of peppermint   Two thick glasses
                                        Brown paper

Measure 2 cupfuls of granulated sugar and put it in a saucepan.

Add 1 cupful of cold water, and set the pan on a hot part of the stove.

When it comes to a boil, look at the clock and boil for about 20 minutes, stirring from time to time.

When you think it's done, try a little, by dropping half a teaspoonful into a glass of cold water.

If it is done it will get stringy and hard in the water.

When you are sure that it is ready, take the pan from the stove, and pour the syrup into two glasses.

Pour $\frac{1}{2}$ teaspoonful of peppermint extract at once into each glass and let each child stir the mixture in his glass rapidly with a teaspoon until the syrup gets thick and creamy white.

Have a large flat sheet of brown wrapping

paper ready on your kitchen table and onto this drop little round dabs of the mixture as rapidly as possible.

Don't let the mixture get too cool and stiff by stirring it longer than necessary.

When entirely hard and cold, the peppermints can be lifted off with a knife.

This makes about half a pound.

CPSIA information can be obtained
at www.ICGtesting.com
Printed in the USA
JSHW041006040821
17551JS00003B/310